And That's How It Went

And That's How It Went

a year's end guide for journaling 2020

CURIOUS CROW BOOKS

First published in 2020 by Curious Crow Books

Victoria Australia

ISBN 978-0-9805249-4-9

Copyright Tor Roxburgh 2020

The moral right of the author has been asserted. All rights reserved. Any person or organisation wanting to copy, store or transmit material contained in this book needs permission in writing from Curious Crow Books.

Design, illustration and typesetting: Holly Dunn

www.torroxburgh.com

How to use this journal

Dear Fellow Traveller in the year 2020,

Welcome to 'That's How It Went'!

If you are anything like me, you fully intended to keep a journal this year but life got in the way. It isn't too late. I've assembled a summary of some of the world's most significant events to frame your story. All you need to do to have a personal history of the year is add something about your life.

You can use this journal to recreate your year. I've added some writing prompts for each week to help you remember what happened and recall how things felt. You might also like to check back through your digital footsteps to help you along the way.

There are bonus prompts at the end of the journal if you need a few extra.

As you work through the journal, try checking back on your social media feed, your music apps, the podcasts you listened to, the books you read, the television you watched, the events in your calendar and the photos on your phone.

If you find there isn't room for everything you have to say, grab a notebook and keep writing.

Your future self will be glad you did.

Your friend in journaling,

Tor Roxburgh

PS It was a big year – a very big year. I've focused on events in Australia and the United States but have tried to include some significant global events. If I haven't paid enough attention to your country, please forgive me and fill in those blanks when you write your story. TR ♥

30 Dec 2019 - 5 Jan 2020

The wheel of the calendar turns as the old year ends and the new begins.

The Globe: China reports cases of 'viral pneumonia' in Wuhan. The World Health Organisation warns about risk from a new acute respiratory infection. Civil rights protests in Hong Kong intensify.

In Australia: All states are alight with fierce bushfires that have expended more than 65 per cent of the nation's emissions budget. The Prime Minister remains in the doghouse for holidaying during the crisis. The Federal Government mobilises the army. The navy rescues 4,000 people from a fire-ringed beach. Penrith, near Sydney, records the hottest temperature on Earth at 48.9 deg C (~120 deg F).

In the United States: The nation sends additional troops to Baghdad in response to protesters storming the US embassy. The US attacks two Iraqi targets it believes are linked to Iran. Julian Castro suspends his presidential campaign.

Prompt: Describe your New Year: Where were you? Who were you with? What were you doing? Describe where you were living in January: What did it look like? How did you feel about your physical surroundings?

6 Jan - 12 Jan 2020

The year has scarcely begun but much has happened. The big story – the illness in China – is still quite small.

The Globe: China identifies the pathogen causing the mystery sickness in Wuhan as a novel coronavirus. It shares the genetic sequence with the World Health Organisation. The virus causes its first death. The Duke and Duchess of Sussex quit their jobs. In Taiwan, President Tsai Ing-wen wins another term. A Ukrainian flight crashes in Iran and kills all on board.

In Australia: Comedian Celeste Barber raises around AU$50 million for her state's fire service and there are estimates that a billion animals have died, with extinction threatening others.

In the United States: Puerto Rico experiences a 6.4 magnitude earthquake. The American Cancer Society confirms that cancer mortality rates are continuing to decline. A teenage intern at NASA discovers a planet.

Prompt: Did you hear about the sickness in China? Did you imagine it would have an impact on you? Describe whether you shared any fears out loud and whether you felt embarrassed in case you were overreacting.

13 Jan - 19 Jan 2020

The religious wheel turns as Hindus celebrate the Lohri, Makar Sankranti, and Pongal festivals this week.

The Globe: Thailand and Japan report their first cases of novel coronavirus infection. China is yet to find evidence of human-to-human transmission, but the World Health Organisation says it is possible.

In Australia: The bushfires press on and the state of New South Wales declares a Natural Disaster for 80 local government areas.

In the United States: Cory Booker leaves the presidential race. Microsoft commits to offsetting its lifetime carbon footprint by 2050. A Major Disaster is declared in Puerto Rico in response to last week's earthquake. Acting on worries about the novel coronavirus, the CDC starts checking passengers from Wuhan.

Prompt: What were your hopes, dreams, and resolutions for 2020? Describe why those ideas were important to you and what experiences drove them.

20 Jan - 26 Jan 2020

The wheel of the calendar turns as China farewells the year of the Pig and welcomes the Rat.

The Globe: The progressive judge, Katerina Sakellaropoulou, is the first female president of Greece. The World Health Organisation sends a mission to China as it begins planning for ways to assess therapies and control the new disease. Chinese officials lockdown Wuhan, make masks mandatory, and confirm human-to-human transmission of the virus. Cases appear in France and begin to be reported across Asia.

In Australia: The first case of coronavirus infection is reported. The bushfires continue burning. At week's end some celebrate Australia Day, but its date remains controversial in the nation's race relations.

In the United States: The week begins with Martin Luther King Junior's birthday. The US reports its first coronavirus infection and Orange County declares a State of Emergency in response to the virus.

Prompt: This week feels like a cusp, where we hesitate before stepping beyond our experiential innocence into a year of trouble. What were the markers in your life, signalling that things were different? What was knocking on your door?

27 Jan - 2 Feb 2020

The religious wheel turns as Hindus celebrate the Basant Panchami Festival. The world begins counting: the Earth's hottest January, the first 100 people dying from the virus, and fewer than 100 cases outside China.

The Globe: The United Kingdom withdraws from the European Union. Israel's Prime Minister is indicted on corruption charges. China extends the national holiday, reducing the movement of people. The World Health Organisation declares a Public Health Emergency of International Concern and ships out the first coronavirus diagnostic kits. In Italy, 7000 people are held on the Costa cruise ship because illness is suspected. Russia closes its border with China.

In Australia: The Federal Government closes its border to mainland China. The Peter Doherty Institute grows and then shares samples of the coronavirus. States of Emergency are declared across the nation. Bushfires continue to burn.

In the United States: The Health and Human Services Secretary declares a public health emergency for the entire nation in response to the virus. The Coronavirus Task Force is formed and the CDC orders Americans returning from Wuhan into quarantine. A day later, the President closes the border to travellers from China.

Prompt: Your future self will want to know about your homelife at this time. Who were you living with? Were you single or deeply-partnered or on the edge of one or the other? Or was the story quite different?

3 Feb - 9 Feb 2020

The world's wheel continues counting numbers as Antarctica's hottest known daily temperature is recorded.

The Globe: Infections grow, but 99 per cent are contained in China, with just 176 cases in the rest of the world. Many grieve the death from coronavirus of Dr Li Wenliang, the Chinese COVID19 whistle blower. The World Health Organisation discusses whether asymptomatic patients can infect others. The Diamond Princess cruise ship is quarantined off the coast of Yokohama, Japan. A Thai soldier kills 29 people in a shopping centre.

In Australia: Australia hears that more than 70 nations have offered help during the bushfire crisis. Western Australia declares an emergency situation as Cyclone Damien damages homes.

In the United States: Christina Koch sets a record for the longest continuous spaceflight by a woman. The US President is acquitted by the Senate at his impeachment trial. No one notices the first coronavirus death until a tissue sample is tested in April.

Prompt: Describe some of the individuals in your extended family. Include something about the most recent encounters you had with them early in 2020. Did you resolve to improve or loosen any of these relationships this year? In hindsight are those thoughts sitting comfortably?

10 Feb - 16 Feb 2020

The religious wheel turns as Jews celebrate the ecological awareness holiday Tu B'Shvat. The world hits another milestone with global deaths reaching 1000.

The Globe: The World Health Organisation names the novel coronavirus disease "COVID19", gathers hundreds of experts to work on the problem, and works with Silicon Valley on the informational challenges. The cruise ship Westerdam docks in Cambodia after being turned away by five countries due to contagion fears. A new species of tyrannosaur is discovered in Canada.

In Australia: Some National Party politicians argue against climate change policies and advocate funding for coal mines. The Prime Minister resists calls for a referendum on the constitutional recognition of Indigenous Australians.

In the United States: Illinois is the first state with the capacity to test for coronavirus. Andrew Yang, an advocate for the idea of a universal basic income, drops out of the Democratic presidential race.

Prompt: With the disease named and the first, but still only slightly, alarming number of deaths, COVID19 was probably at the edge of your attention. Describe what was in focus: Was there a family wedding? Were you thinking about work? Did you have assignments? Did you have special projects? Were you politically active?

17 Feb - 23 Feb 2020

The calendar arrives at Presidents' Day in the United States and the religious wheel turns as Hindus celebrate Maha Shivaratri.

The Globe: The World Health Organisation deploys special envoys to advise on large-scale public health measures to tackle the coronavirus problem.

In Australia: The Federal Government publishes its first novel coronavirus plan. General Motors decides to leave Australia and kill off the Holden brand.

In the United States: MIT uses artificial intelligence to discover that the diabetes drug halicin can be used as an antibiotic. A black man, Ahmaud Arbery, is shot while jogging by local white men, signalling a tragedy for a family – and for a nation struggling with race relations.

Prompt: If we hadn't had a pandemic and a race relations crisis this year we would probably be talking about data and artificial intelligence. Your future self will want to know your thoughts about these themes.

24 Feb – 1 Mar 2020

The seasons turn: summer to autumn in the Southern Hemisphere; winter to spring in the Northern Hemisphere. As the religious wheel shifts, Lent begins for Christians. The world counts cases: now more outside China than within.

The Globe: There is COVID19 in every continent except Antarctica. Dr Mahathir Mohamad resigns as Malaysia's Prime Minister. Muhyiddin Yassin is his successor. The 2020 locust plague arrives in nine African countries. There are global shortages of personal protective equipment. Global miner Rio Tinto pledges net zero carbon emissions by 2050.

In Australia: Western Australia reports Australia's first novel coronavirus death. There are floods in New South Wales. Leaders argue about whether left- or right-wing extremists pose a greater risk.

In the United States: Harvey Weinstein is convicted of rape and sexual assault. The first two people die from COVID19. In subsequent months, the first death is revised back to February 6. The Health and Human Services Secretary says the novel coronavirus poses a low risk. Pete Buttigieg drops out of the US presidential race.

Prompt: Describe this week's change of seasons in your location. Include some of the sights and smells. Inspired by the start of Lent and the theme of preparation, describe some of the important preparations you would have been making at this time to mitigate your COVID19 risks.

2 Mar - 8 Mar 2020

The world continues counting milestones as its COVID19 cases surpass 100,000.

The Globe: China's pollution levels drop because of disease containment measures. Shortages and perceived shortages grip the world. People start panic buying, especially toilet paper. Iran temporarily releases 54,000 prisoners to stop the spread of COVID19. Mustafa al-Kadhimi becomes Iraq's Prime Minister.

In Australia: The nation reports the first case of community transmission of COVID19. The country's bushfires have been contained. The Federal Government agrees to meet half the increased health costs of patients with COVID19. Australians are urged to show restraint when buying toilet paper.

In the United States: The House of Representatives passes a US$8.3 billion package to respond to COVID19. The CDC allows testing for anyone with a doctor's order. New York and a number of states declare emergencies in response to COVID19. Michael Bloomberg and Elizabeth Warren drop out of the Democratic presidential race.

Prompt: Were you beginning to worry about shortages? What were you buying? What were you avoiding? Why was everyone so worried about toilet paper: is the answer obvious or symbolic of something else?

9 Mar - 15 Mar 2020

The religious wheel turns as Hindus celebrate Holi and Jews celebrate Purim. The world watches as the US reaches 1000 COVID19 cases.

The Globe: Europe is the new epicentre of the 'pandemic', a word which the World Health Organisation finally endorses. The working from home movement accelerates as Google and Twitter switch to remote work for their employees. A new, tiny dinosaur skeleton is discovered in a piece of amber. Wild white stork chicks hatch in Britain for the first time since the year 1416.

In Australia: Tom Hanks and Rita Wilson test positive while visiting Australia. A new National Cabinet restricts mass gatherings to 500 people. The Federal Government funds a telehealth system and announces an AU$17.6 billion stimulus package.

In the United States: The President declares a national emergency, suspends travel from 26 European countries, and announces a scheme to aid vaccine development. Washington DC and 10 more states declare COVID19-related emergencies. The Dow Jones experiences its sharpest drop ever. Breonna Taylor is shot in her bed by police.

Prompt: This week was full of abrupt events and the situation was evolving rapidly. Describe how you were coping with the sudden changes. Were you in lockdown? Were you preparing for lockdown? What was going on in the place where you live? What freedoms were curtailed and how did you view the restrictions?

16 Mar – 22 Mar 2020

The wheel of the calendar turns to St Patrick's Day and the equinox balances the length of day and night. The world continues marking milestones as the global death toll passes 10,000.

The Globe: New Zealand closes its border. Italy's death toll surpasses China's. China has no new infections. The ambition of 'flattening the curve' enters the pandemic conversation. About 50 countries have travel bans to curb COVID19. The World Health Organisation launches an international clinical trial system for treatments and criticises the US President for calling COVID19 the "Chinese Virus". Eurovision is cancelled.

In Australia: The Federal Government closes the border and effectively doubles unemployment payments. Infected passengers disembark from the Ruby Princess. The National Cabinet imposes COVID19 restrictions and cancels ANZAC Day celebrations. Tasmania closes its border and states and territories announce lockdowns.

In the United States: The coronavirus is present in all 50 states. The President invokes the Defence Production Act. New York has more than 15,000 cases of COVID19. Northern Californians are ordered to shelter in place for three weeks. The US/Canada border closes indefinitely.

Prompt: There was a moment in March when I woke up crying because the world's ordinary story had disappeared. Describe one of your emotional moments this year. Was it about the world's life, or your life, or the life of someone you love?

23 Mar – 29 Mar 2020

The world's wheel turns as the US takes the lead in confirmed cases of COVID19.

The Globe: With just 205 cases, New Zealand confines citizens to their homes, eventually eliminating the virus. Japan postpones the Olympics. India declares a 21-day lockdown, creating a crisis for day workers. Prince Charles is diagnosed with COVID19. The World Health Organisation advises on setting up treatment centres. The UK Prime Minister tests positive to COVID19.

In Australia: Thousands queue for welfare. The Federal Government forbids Australians from leaving the country. The National Cabinet announces a six-month moratorium on evictions. Domestic borders tighten. Australians are working remotely and panic buying vegetables and seeds.

In the United States: The President signs a US$2 trillion stimulus bill. Just under half of the population is experiencing local lockdown measures. Disaster declarations in response to the pandemic are widespread. The New York Stock Exchange closes it trading floor in response to COVID19.

Prompt: In the coming months the patterns of lockdowns diverge. During these few weeks it felt as though we were sharing some of the hardship as a global community. Your future self will want to read about the early days of your first lockdown and how your community reacted.

30 Mar – 5 Apr 2020

The religious wheel turns as Hindus celebrate Ram Navami and China celebrates the Qingming Festival, also known as Tomb Sweeping Day. The coronavirus count passes another milestone as more than 50,000 people have died.

The Globe: The World Health Organisation warns of COVID19 misinformation, launches a multilingual chatbot, and ships around two million items of protective equipment to 74 countries. It also confirms that symptomatic, pre-symptomatic and asymptomatic people can transmit the virus.

In Australia: The Federal Government announces its third stimulus package, introducing a new scheme that pays businesses AU$1500 per employee a fortnight to maintain employment. Western Australia closes its domestic border.

In the United States: New York sets a record of 12,000 COVID19 cases in a single day. The CDC recommends wearing non-surgical masks in public. Some 91 per cent of Americans are affected by stay-at-home orders. The death toll exceeds 5000 people. COVID19-related disaster declarations continue to be announced.

Prompt: It feels as though this week introduces all sorts of unfamiliar behaviours such as restrictions on movement and mask-wearing. What was going in your life? Were you wearing a mask at the start of April? What did it look like? Were you obsessively washing hands? Were you sanitising? Were you making your own sanitiser?

6 Apr - 12 Apr 2020

The religious wheel turns to a significant week for Christians as Lent ends and Good Friday and Easter Sunday arrive; and for Jews too as they celebrate Pesach (Passover). The world reaches a shocking milestone as the number of COVID19 deaths reaches 100,000.

The Globe: The Pope suggests the coronavirus may be one of nature's responses to climate change. The Wuhan lockdown ends as China succeeds in suppressing the virus. The United Nations launches a COVID19 supply chain taskforce.

In Australia: Perth experiences its hottest April weather at 39.5 deg C (~103.1 deg F) as cold, rainy weather blasts the nation's south-east. The High Court quashes Cardinal George Pell's convictions for child sexual abuse.

In the United States: Joe Biden becomes the presumptive Democratic presidential nominee after Bernie Sanders suspends his campaign. Evidence emerges that New York's first COVID19 cases came from Europe. The disease case count surpasses 400,000. States continue announcing major disasters in response to the pandemic.

Prompt: This week is significant for two of the major religions. Describe any of the rituals that you were involved in this week. If you are an atheist or follow a different faith, your future self might enjoy reading about where you found your transcendent and spiritual moments in the first quarter of 2020.

13 Apr - 19 Apr 2020

The religious wheel turns as Christians farewell Easter and Hindus celebrate Baisakhi.

The Globe: The World Health Organisation organises a collaboration to develop a coronavirus vaccine. New Zealand's Prime Minister and cabinet volunteer for a pay cut. President Moon Jae-in wins the South Korean elections. In Canada, a man kills 22 people. The UK Prime Minister leaves hospital after treatment for COVID19. Over 100 countries request help from the International Monetary Fund. The sale of puzzles jumps.

In Australia: The Artania cruise ship departs Perth three weeks after a fraught docking process. The Federal Government subsidises airlines to continue domestic flights.

In the United States: The director of the National Institute of Allergy and Infectious Diseases says the curve is flattening. The media begins talking about a roadmap for re-opening the nation. The US halts funding to the World Health Organisation.

Prompt: This week feels as though it is full of cooperation and collective effort (with a notable exception). There have been inspiring moments this year. Describe some of yours.

20 Apr – 26 Apr 2020

The religious wheel turns, bringing us to Yom Hashoah, Holocaust Remembrance Day. Muslims begin fasting for Ramadan.

The Globe: The world begins to discuss 'Long COVID'. There are early indications that a drug called Remdesivir may help patients with severe COVID19. Taiwan effectively eliminates the coronavirus with a mask-led, no-lockdown approach. Images of mass graves in Brazil appear in the media. The Iranian President calls for equal rights for men and women. The Sudan Council of Ministers criminalises female genital mutilation.

In Australia: Western Australia, Queensland, South Australia, and the Northern Territory report no new cases, but Tasmania experiences an outbreak. The community celebrates ANZAC Day from driveways. The Federal Government launches COVIDSafe – a digital tracing app.

In the United States: The President suggests investigating whether COVID19 patients could benefit from being injected with disinfectant. His comments are condemned by doctors and scientists. Five states re-open. A tissue sample is examined that resets the date of the first US death to early February.

Prompt: There was a lot of fear at this stage in the year. How were you feeling? Do you have children who wanted to know what was going on? What were your feelings about the elderly members of your family? What about your own vulnerabilities?

27 Apr - 3 May 2020

The season changes from wet to dry in the north of Australia.

The Globe: New Zealand achieves zero cases of community transmission and maintains zero for 100-plus days. Across the world, many countries begin planning to ease restrictions. Canada restricts the sale of 1500 firearm models.

In Australia: The final blaze in the Western Australian fire season is extinguished. The number of coronavirus cases in Australia appears to be falling.

In the United States: The US exceeds a million cases of COVID19. Armed protesters storm the Michigan Capitol building. Eleven more states re-open.

Prompt: Your future self will want to know what your thoughts were about the anti-lockdown, anti-restriction protests and whether your thoughts changed as the year progressed. Describe the attitudes in your community.

4 May – 10 May 2020

The world's wheel turns to remembering WWII as VE Day recalls the allied victory in Europe.

The Globe: UK and Kenyan scientists discover a microbe that protects mosquitoes from malaria, offering a pathway to control the disease. Ireland raises US$2 million for the Navajo and Hopi nations during the pandemic in return for indigenous Americans' help during the 1847 famine.

In Australia: The National Cabinet agrees to a three-step roadmap to lift lockdown. The Chief Medical Officer reports that the nation's death rate from COVID19 is "much, much lower than comparable countries".

In the United States: Twelve more states re-open. The President reverses an earlier statement about disbanding the Coronavirus Taskforce. Department store chain Neiman Marcus files for bankruptcy.

Prompt: While there is bad news this week, the mood seems to be optimistic with lots of governments re-opening or planning to re-open. On the domestic front, plans can sustain us through hard times. What were you looking forward to? What ideas did you have that were awaiting a little bit more freedom?

11 May - 17 May 2020

The religious wheel turns as Jews celebrate Lag B'Omer.

The Globe: Pro-democracy rallies resume after almost all of Hong Kong's patients with COVID19 have recovered. In Israel the Netanyahu-Gantz unity government is sworn in. The World Health Organisation releases a scientific brief on multisystem inflammatory syndrome in child and adolescent COVID19 patients.

In Australia: Privacy legislation for the COVIDSafe app passes through Federal Parliament. International students face poverty and are forced to resort to charity after losing their casual work.

In the United States: The US department store JC Penney files for bankruptcy. Ten more states re-open.

Prompt: Describe your social life at this point in the year. Your future self will want to be reminded about how you were connecting with friends, colleagues, and family. Was it Zoom or WhatsApp or texts? Was it old-school? Face-to-face conversations? Phone calls? Letters?

18 May – 24 May 2020

The religious wheel turns as Ramadan ends and Muslims enjoy breaking their fast during the Eid al-Fitr celebration.

The Globe: The UK Prime Minister refuses to sack his chief advisor despite evidence he broke lockdown rules. Cambridge University cancels face-to-face learning until mid-2021. A Pakistani plane crashes, killing 22 people. Beijing seeks to impose national security legislation on Hong Kong.

In Australia: The nation records 100 COVID19 deaths. The Chief Medical Officer is ignored when he says that there is no reason to close state borders. Six million people have downloaded the COVIDSafe tracing app. Victoria and New South Wales are easing restrictions.

In the United States: The US records more than 1.5 million cases of COVID19. Four more states re-open.

Prompt: This year has highlighted tensions between acting as a unified nation and the desire of states and territories to make their own decisions for their own communities. How have those tensions impacted your life? Are there parallel tensions in your family life?

25 May - 31 May 2020

The world arrives at a week fraught with protests, but there is good news too.

The Globe: New Zealand marks five days with no new COVID19 cases. Costa Rica legalises same-sex marriage. The Iranian President seeks legislation to prevent violence against women. The evidential tide turns against chloroquine and hydroxychloroquine as a treatment for COVID19. Beijing approves national security legislation for Hong Kong. The demand for flour and baking ingredients grows.

In Australia: Australia continues to experience a run on vegetable seedlings, seeds, and chooks. The Prime Minister says the National Cabinet model will be made permanent. There is a small COVID19 outbreak in Victoria's hotel quarantine system.

In the United States: The US recalls the fallen on Memorial Day, during a tumultuous week. George Floyd is killed during an arrest. Black Lives Matter protests erupt across the US. The President threatens to deploy the military. Statues are torn down. The nation surpasses 100,000 COVID19 deaths but continues to re-open. Twitter tags the US President's tweets. The SpaceX Falcon 9 launches a mission to the International Space Station.

Prompt: Your future self will want to know what you thought about race relations in 2020 and what was going on in your neighbourhood and in your family. What were your insights? Has your thinking evolved over the year?

1 Jun - 7 Jun 2020

The seasons turn: autumn to winter in the Southern Hemisphere; spring to summer in the Northern Hemisphere.

The Globe: *The Lancet* reports that wearing face masks reduces person-to-person transmission of COVID19. The Prime Minister of Armenia tests positive to the disease. The World Health Organisation reports the lowest number of new cases in Europe since March 22. George Floyd's death leads to protests around the world.

In Australia: Black Lives Matter protests erupt in Australia. There is anguished debate about street protests during the pandemic.

In the United States: National Guard troops clear Black Lives Matter demonstrators to create a presidential photo opportunity. A Kentucky police chief kneels with Black Lives Matter protesters. The Mayor of Washington DC renames a street 'Black Lives Matter Plaza', painting the slogan on the road's surface. Four Minnesota officers are charged in relation to Floyd's death.

Prompt: It's six months into the year and tensions are high. Have you revised your ambitions for 2020 and has there been any shift in your values? What about your loved ones' values?

8 Jun – 14 Jun 2020

The wheel of the calendar turns and there are 200 days remaining before the end of the year.

The Globe: Beijing goes into lockdown to deal with a COVID19 outbreak. Eighty-one people are killed in a Boko Haram attack in Nigeria. There are protests in Lebanon after the currency collapses.

In Australia: The nation is averaging fewer than 10 cases a day. The Prime Minister reiterates Australia's ambition to suppress not eliminate COVID19. The Black Lives Matter protests continue to be a subject of public health debate in government.

In the United States: Minneapolis City councillors want to create an alternative policing model. The 'defund the police' concept gains advocates and detractors and is widely misunderstood to mean abolishing the police. Rayshard Brooks is killed by police in a restaurant carpark in Atlanta.

Prompt: It is a year for contentious ideas like universal basic income and defunding the police. What do you think? And what are your big ideas this year? Events will have triggered some deep and personal thoughts about life.

15 Jun - 21 Jun 2020

The Southern Hemisphere reaches the winter solstice: the shortest day of the year. The Northern Hemisphere marks the summer solstice: the longest day of the year. Globally, COVID19 cases surpass 8.5 million.

The Globe: Hydroxychloroquine fails to show it can reduce mortality for hospitalised COVID19 patients. In contrast, Dexamethasone is shown to cut death by a third in patients on ventilators or receiving oxygen in hospital. The President of Honduras tests positive. India reports the death of 20 soldiers in a violent clash with Chinese soldiers. The Beijing outbreak is contained.

In Australia: The nation's COVID19 case count is low, but there is a second hotel quarantine outbreak in Melbourne. The Victorian Government tightens restrictions for indoor and outdoor numbers. Australia experiences a major cyber attack.

In the United States: The Food and Drug Administration revokes the emergency use authorisation for Chloroquine and Hydroxychloroquine for COVID19 patients. The Supreme Court finds that discrimination against workers based on sexual orientation and gender identity is unlawful.

Prompt: What were you doing around the time of the solstice and how did the length of the day impact your daily life? Did the time of year make the pandemic harder or easier?

22 Jun - 28 Jun 2020

The religious wheel falters for some Muslims as Saudi Arabia announces that the Hajj is closed to international pilgrims.

The Globe: Brazil experiences more than 20,000 COVID19 cases in 24 hours. Micheál Martin becomes the Prime Minister of Ireland.

In Australia: Case numbers continue to rise from a low base and now average 33 a day. Victorians hear that some quarantined travellers have resisted testing. Supermarkets re-introduce restrictions on toilet paper sales.

In the United States: Case numbers continue to climb. The number of young people getting infected is increasing. Experts, universities, governments, collages, schools, students, and families all grapple with the question of face-to-face classes and remote learning.

Prompt: Are you working from home? If you have children, are they studying at home? Are you loving being homebound or hating it? What was going on in your daily life at this point? The details are important in remembering what your year was like.

29 Jun - 5 Jul 2020

The year turns to Independence Day in the United States. The world marks another milestone as the coronavirus death toll reaches 500,000.

The Globe: China approves a COVID19 vaccine for its military, but the world expresses concern about a lack of transparency in its approval system. Europe opens its borders to 15 non-European Union countries but excludes the US. India bans TikTok.

In Australia: A second wave of COVID19 is worsening. The Victorian Government re-introduces local lockdowns in 10 postcodes, locks down public housing towers with known cases, and announces an inquiry into the hotel quarantine system.

In the United States: Washington commences efforts to rescind Hong Kong's special trading status. Socialite Ghislaine Maxwell is arrested and charged with crimes relating to sexual abuse connected to her association with Jeffrey Epstein. Sixteen states halt their reopening plans because of a COVID19 case surge. Kanye West announces that he is running for President.

Prompt: The week feels fragmented as different countries, cities, states, and belief systems head in diverse directions. Was the fragmentation touching you? Your future self will want to know about how this mood impacted your family and the relationships within your community.

6 Jul - 12 Jul 2020

The world's wheel turns as thoughts focus on the reality of COVID19's forceful second waves.

The Globe: The President of Brazil and the interim President of Bolivia test positive for COVID19. The pandemic causes a drop in consumption and the largest drop of Greenhouse gas emissions in history.

In Australia: The nation's second wave worsens and domestic borders close, cutting off Victorians. Stay-at-home rules return and a five-month 'Ring of Steel' border is placed between Melbourne and regional Victoria.

In the United States: The US surpasses 3 million cases of COVID19. The nation gives formal notice of its withdrawal from the World Health Organisation. The Supreme Court rules that New York prosecutors can examine the President's financial records. Almost a third of Americans with home loans fail to make payments this month.

Prompt: This week the world feels justifiably anxious, particularly about finances. Lockdowns hit employment hard and people across the globe are having money trouble. Your future self will want to be reminded about how you felt and whether you were enduring financial problems.

13 Jul - 19 Jul 2020

The calendar week brings Juneteenth, a day celebrating the emancipation of slaves in the United States. The world's wheel turns to a grim milestone as the globe records a million cases in just 100 hours.

The Globe: The total number of cases passes 13 million. The United Nations warns of a vast increase in chronic hunger resulting from the pandemic. Nations collaborate on access to COVID19 vaccines. Save the Children suggests that 10 million children may never go back to school post-pandemic.

In Australia: It is mandatory to wear masks in the city of Melbourne as the Victorian Government continues its vigorous public health measures to subdue the second wave.

In the United States: Civil rights leader John Lewis dies. Washington engages in a struggle with the CDC to manage patient data. The Administration wants schools to open and there is talk of linking school reopening to stimulus money. The Twitter accounts of corporate leaders and politicians are hacked in a Bitcoin scam.

_____
_____
_____
_____
_____
_____
_____
_____
_____
_____
_____
_____
_____
_____

Prompt: This week feels as though the themes of freedom and justice are calling us. They can be global ideas or something much closer to home. Describe the state of justice and equity in your home. Has the pandemic changed gender relationships in your life? What about generational relationships?

20 Jul - 26 Jul 2020

This week the world's climate and pandemic problems compete for attention.

The Globe: Imperial College London finds that in good locations, offshore wind is cheap enough to generate income for consumers. Mexico surpasses 40,000 deaths with grim scenes of raw graves.

In Australia: The New South Wales government declares a natural disaster after storms and floods. The Deputy Chief Medical Officer reports a rise in infections in New South Wales and Victoria. The Victorian Government examines security problems in Melbourne's hotel quarantine system.

In the United States: Massachusetts makes Juneteenth a holiday, as racial unrest continues across the US. The wildfire season is underway. The Pine Gulch Fire ignites after a lightning strike in Colorado and Hurricane Hanna hits Texas. The US surpasses 4 million cases of COVID19.

Prompt: There was fear and dismay in the early days of the pandemic. Has it returned? Were you worrying about illness this week? About death? Has your working life put you at risk? Describe the risks you face and what thoughts you've had about mortality.

27 Jul - 2 Aug 2020

The religious wheel turns as Muslims celebrate Eid ul Adha (the Festival of Sacrifice) and Jews fast on Tisha B'Av (to remember tragic days in Jewish history). The world struggles to come to terms with the worsening pandemic.

The Globe: The President of Belarus tests positive for COVID19. The price of gold hits a new high. Former Malaysian Prime Minister Datuk Seri Najib Razak is found guilty of theft. Costa Rica has reversed rainforest deforestation, returning 60 per cent of the land to forest.

In Australia: The Australian second wave is worsening. In one day, Victoria has a high of 723 new cases of COVID19, a number close to the UK's daily case count. Melbourne's lockdown is tightened and mandatory mask wearing is extended to the entire State.

In the United States: Phoenix, Delaware, Maryland, New Hampshire, and New Jersey experience their hottest July – with Connecticut, Pennsylvania, and Virginia tying on their hottest July. Florida experiences its hottest year in recorded history. The Red Salmon Complex fire ignites in California. The US surpasses 150,000 COVID19 deaths. The US$600 per week Cares Act pandemic aid expires. The majority of 18- to 29-year-olds are living with their parents. Tropical storm Isaias reaches Puerto Rico.

Prompt: This week leans towards themes in the natural word: destruction and reforestation. For many, 2020's pandemic and climate change concerns have heightened their emotional relationship with the natural world. Describe how the year has impacted your relationship with nature. Has it led to new resolutions? New habits?

3 Aug - 9 Aug 2020

The religious wheel turns as Hindus celebrate Raksha Bandhan, a festival of brotherhood and love and Jews focus on love during Tu B'Av.

The Globe: The Beirut Port explosion in Lebanon kills 190 people. The Prime Minister of Kosovo tests positive for COVID19. Alexander Lukashenko claims victory in the disputed Belarus elections. Bolivia cancels both online and in person school for 2020. Brazil surpasses 100,000 deaths.

In Australia: The second wave peaks, a fact that won't be known for some time yet. The New South Wales government mops up after storms and floods.

In the United States: The US surpasses 5 million COVID19 cases. The Sturgis Motorcycle Rally in South Dakota results in 290 cases in 12 states. An outbreak at a summer camp in Georgia results in 2,060 cases. Hurricane Isaias hits North Carolina. SpaceX delivers two astronauts back to Earth.

_____
_____
_____
_____
_____
_____
_____
_____
_____
_____
_____
_____
_____
_____

Prompt: The week leans towards love. Describe who comes to mind when you think of brotherhood and sisterhood. Your future self will be extremely interested in where your heart lies this year. Remind yourself about what your loved ones were doing and where they were living.

10 Aug - 16 Aug 2020

The religious wheel turns as Hindus celebrate Krishna Janmashtami.

The Globe: New Zealand experiences an outbreak of COVID19 after more than 100 infection-free days. Prime Minister Hassan Diab resigns in Lebanon. Israel and the United Arab Emirates move towards peaceful relations. Svetlana Tikhanovskaya claims electoral victory in Belarus. A new species of theropod dinosaur is discovered on the Isle of Wight.

In Australia: Evidence emerges that women and young people are the hardest hit by the pandemic's economic consequences. Global miner BHP withdraws support for Australia's use of carryover credits to reach its Paris climate commitments.

In the United States: Kamala Harris is chosen as the Democratic vice-presidential nominee. Death Valley California records 129.9 deg F (54.4 deg C). The wildfire season rages in California and Oregon. The August Complex wildfire becomes the largest complex fire on record in California and the State's first 'gigafire', the name for a blaze that burns more than a million acres (~400,000 hectares).

Prompt: In the gravity of the global situation, the small concerns of everyday life still matter. For many people not being able to visit the barber, hairdresser or beautician became surprisingly hard. Describe whether you have had to miss out on the small acts of self-care that were routine in 2019. Why do you think those things matter?

17 Aug - 23 Aug 2020

The religious wheel turns as Muslims celebrate Muharram, the Islamic New Year while Hindus celebrate Ganesh Chaturthi and Onam, and Hindu women enjoy Hartalika Teej.

The Globe: The Russian opposition leader, Alexei Navalny, falls ill en-route from Siberia to Moscow, lapsing into a coma. Poisoning is suspected. He is flown to Berlin for treatment.

In Australia: Evidence emerges that 90 per cent of Victoria's second wave cases result from the virus escaping the returned traveller hotel quarantine system. The use of private security firms to police that system comes into focus. The rest of Australia is relatively virus-free.

In the United States: Joe Biden formally accepts the Democratic presidential nomination. A study finds that more than 93 per cent of Black Lives Matter demonstrations have been peaceful. More major fires ignite in California and the State declares a disaster. The states of Oregon and Washington declare fire-related emergencies. Iowa experiences the most expensive storm in US history.

Prompt: Fire has bookended 2020. Australia entered the year with an horrific fire season and the United States is ending the year in a wildfire season of shocking proportions. Have you been impacted by these fire seasons or by extreme weather? Your future self will want to know your thoughts about the causes and whether climate change was concerning you.

24 Aug - 30 Aug 2020

On the cusp of the change of seasons, there is worry in the Northern Hemisphere about the winter ahead and whether populations will face seasonal influenza on top of coronavirus.

The Globe: Hong Kong confirms the first case of COVID19 reinfection. Police detain 20 journalists in Belarus. In New Zealand, Australian right-wing terrorist Brenton Tarrant is jailed for life. The Japanese Prime Minister resigns due to ill health. The World Health Organisation declares Africa polio-free. A Japanese company successfully tests a piloted flying car.

In Australia: The Victorian Government introduces a bill to extend its COVID19 emergency from 6 to 12 months. The proposal is widely misunderstood to mean the state wants to lock down the population for a year. Case numbers are dropping but lockdown remains in place and Melburnians struggle with their mental health.

In the United States: Donald Trump accepts the Republican presidential nomination. The Food and Drug Administration authorises the first COVID19 rapid diagnostic test for emergency use. Hurricane Laura hits South West Louisiana.

Prompt: The struggle to maintain optimism and good mental health has been a theme in 2020 and was particularly challenging for those living in the long Melbourne lockdown. How have you been doing? Describe the everyday ways that you have held onto optimism or been assailed by pessimism.

31 Aug - 6 Sep 2020

The seasons turn: winter to spring in the Southern Hemisphere; summer to fall in the Northern Hemisphere.

The Globe: Russia surpasses a million cases. Germany confirms Alexei Navalny was poisoned with nerve agent Novichok. Religion and State are separated in Sudan after 30 years. The world enjoys the first chord change of John Cage's 639-year-long music composition.

In Australia: The Victorian Government wins an extension to its State of Emergency powers by reducing the timeframe. The phrases 'Dictator Dan' and 'Chairman Dan', referring to Premier Daniel Andrews, get traction during the continuing lockdown. Labor wins the Northern Territory election. Confirmation that Australia is in its first recession in 29 years.

In the United States: August overtakes July as the hottest month on record in Phoenix. LA County records its highest temperature of 121 deg F (49 deg C). More major fires ignite in the states of California and Washington. The US surpasses 6 million cases of COVID19. In the ordinary course of events, all students would have started school this week. The Black Lives Matter protests have been active for 100 days.

Prompt: This week global life feels particularly disrupted and it seems as though people are stretched to their limits. What sort of disruptions have you experienced? Has dating been put on hold? Were your holidays cancelled? Was your education stalled? Did your workplace close? What about plans to have children, visit grandchildren, get married or get divorced?

7 Sep - 13 Sep 2020

The wheel of the calendar turns as Americans celebrate Labor Day.

The Globe: The World Health Organisations reports that there are 34 vaccine candidates in clinical evaluation and 145 in pre-clinical evaluation. Oxford and AstraZeneca resume their vaccine trial in the UK after investigating a reported side-effect.

In Australia: Australia's daily case count drops to 54 – and most are still in Victoria. Police arrest 74 people after two days of lockdown protests.

In the United States: More major fires ignite in California, Washington State, and Oregon. The Almeda Drive fire in Oregon transforms from a brush fire to an urban fire. There are suggestions that presidential officials manipulated a CDC report.

Prompt: The world's events can seem very distant from domestic life. Your future self will want to know about the ordinary things in your life. Describe a typical 2020 day. It could be an amalgam of the walks you've been taking, the meals you've been eating, and the routine conversations you've been having.

14 Sep - 20 Sep 2020

The religious wheel turns as Jews celebrate the new year on Rosh Hashana.

The Globe: Europe's second wave cases rise at a higher rate than during the first wave. Yoshihide Suga is confirmed as Prime Minister of Japan. The President of Guatemala tests positive for COVID19. The German government opens a department store selling used and upcycled goods.

In Australia: The nation's daily COVID19 case count averages 36 new cases of COVID19, the majority are still in Victoria and the State maintains lockdown. A data leak indicates China has collected information on more than 35,000 Australians.

In the United States: Ruth Bader Ginsburg dies, leaving a Supreme Court vacancy. Oregon declares a major disaster in response to fire and winds. Google announces it has offset its lifetime carbon footprint.

Prompt: This is another week where it feels as though the world pauses on the edge of something, waiting to see what will happen. It is an uncomfortable position to be in. Has a feeling of constraint, of impatience, or of waiting factored in your life this year? Describe how you have managed your need for agency and action when there has been little under your control.

21 Sep - 27 Sep 2020

The equinox balances the length of day and night and the religious wheel reaches Yom Kippur as Jews reflect on repentance and atonement.

The Globe: China commits to peak carbon emissions before 2030 and carbon neutrality before 2060. The Canadian Prime Minister confirms his nation's second wave. In Lebanon Prime Minister-designate Mustapha Adib resigns after being unable to form government.

In Australia: Pilot whales beach on Tasmania's shores and about 380 die. Vincent Namatjira's portrait of footballer Adam Goodes wins the Archibald prize.

In the United States: The president chooses Amy Coney Barrett for the Supreme Court vacancy. The US surpasses 7 million COVID19 cases and 200,000 deaths (more than 20 per cent of global deaths). New York's case numbers are growing. The President refuses to commit to a peaceful transfer of power after the US elections.

Prompt: This week feels as though the globe is reminding us that ordinary life does go on and work gets down. Take off those dystopian glasses and describe the things in your life that are fresh and new and good. It might be a new job or a renewed friendship and a new habit you have cultivated.

28 Sep - 4 Oct 2020

The religious wheel turns to the joyful Jewish festival of Sukkot.

The Globe: The global death toll reaches a million. The World Health Organisation confirms that over 100 potential vaccines are being developed. England bans plastic straws, stirring sticks and cotton buds.

In Australia: Pre-poll voting opens in the Australian Capital Territory election. New South Wales enjoys nine days without any locally transmitted cases of COVID19. Victoria is getting close to eliminating community spread of the coronavirus as it continues the lockdown.

In the United States: Cleveland hosts the first presidential debate. The President and 43,752 other Americans test positive for COVID19. Several Californian fires are brought under control or extinguished. New York and Delaware declare disasters in response to tropical storm Isaias.

Prompt: This week's theme feels as though it could be about adjustment to 'COVID Normal' while we wait for vaccines. In the domestic world, puzzles and baking and knitting and digital 'drinks' are still featuring but our natural inclinations have winnowed the options. Describe what new activities you've tried this year and which ones have stuck.

5 Oct - 11 Oct 2020

The religious wheel turns as Jews celebrate Simchat Torah. The pandemic worsens with widespread second waves in the Northern Hemisphere.

The Globe: The number of global cases surpasses 36 million. New Zealand overcomes its August outbreak. Brazil surpasses 5 million cases and India surpasses 7 million cases of COVID19. Canada sets a goal of zero plastic waste by 2030. Ikea announces that it will buy back used furniture for resale and recycling.

In Australia: Tasmanian Devils are reintroduced to mainland Australia for the first time in 3,000 years. For one hour this week the South Australian solar power grid meets 100 per cent of the State's needs.

In the United States: Salt Lake City hosts the vice-presidential debate. The second presidential debate is cancelled due to the President's COVID19 illness. The US surpasses 7.5 million cases and the President delays stimulus talks until after election day.

Prompt: The week it feels as though whatever we were waiting for a few weeks ago, it's happened. The world acted – or didn't act – and the pandemic accelerated. An overview of the year gives a bleak picture, but some of our responses improved our lives. Have you started a business this year? Embarked on a new creative process? Changed jobs? Changed relationships?

12 Oct - 18 Oct 2020

The wheel of the calendar reaches Columbus Day in the United States.

The Globe: Canada celebrates its Thanksgiving Day. China announces it will test all 9 million people in the city of Qingdao. Jacinda Ardern is re-elected as New Zealand Prime Minister. The International Energy Agency announces that the best solar power systems now offer the cheapest electricity in history.

In Australia: The Australian Capital Territory has a COVID-style election day with many people voting early. Victorians experience a tiny, joyful easing of restrictions in one of the longest COVID19 lockdowns in the world, extending Melburnians' 5km (~3mile) travel limit to 25km (~15.5miles).

In the United States: Amy Coney Barrett's Supreme Court confirmation hearing commences. The US surpasses 8 million COVID19 cases, with surges in 17 states. Mask-wearing remains patchy and politically divisive. Johnson & Johnson halts its vaccine trial. Eli Lilly pauses its COVID19 antibody drug trial.

Prompt: Earlier in the year there were suggestions that a vaccine could be ready by year's end despite warnings from experts that it was unlikely. Now there is talk about widespread vaccination not taking place until 2022. What are your thoughts about city living? Describe your plans to make the best of the next 12 to 18 months.

19 Oct - 25 Oct 2020

The religious wheel turns as Hindus celebrate Durga Puja and Dussehra. The world's pandemic milestones continue to climb.

The Globe: Russia surpasses 1.5 million cases of COVID19. Brazil, Argentina, Spain, France, and Colombia surpass a million cases. Poland effectively bans abortion. Honduras becomes the 50th member state to ratify the Treaty on the Prohibition of Nuclear Weapons.

In Australia: The Greens and Labor emerge triumphant in the Australian Capital Territory election. Tasmania lifts its border with South Australia. The Premier of Victoria pauses re-opening while a small outbreak is contained in Melbourne's north.

In the United States: Tennessee hosts a second presidential debate. There are 62 active large fires across Arizona, California, Colorado, Idaho, Missouri, Montana, New Mexico, Oklahoma, Oregon, Utah, Washington, and Wyoming. Around 8,408,603 acres (~3,402,841 hectares) have been burned. Some states are reversing their reopening in response to the renewed COVID19 wave and some are hitting pause.

Prompt: With the pandemic growing, it's more and more likely that you or your family will have been tested for COVID19. Your future self will want to be reminded about what it was like and what led to the decision to get tested. Overall, your future self will want to read about the changes 2020 has wrought in your relationship to your health and wellbeing.

26 Oct – 1 Nov 2020

In the north of Australia the dry season is transitioning to the wet. The calendar reaches Halloween. The religious wheel turns as Muslims celebrate Mawlid al-Nabi, the Prophet's birthday.

The Globe: The UK surpasses a million, France surpasses 1.3 million, Russia surpasses 1.6 million, Brazil surpasses 5.5 million, and India surpasses 8 million cases of COVID19. As European countries re-enter lockdown, shoppers race for pasta, toilet paper and the other staples. An earthquake hits Greece and Turkey. Japan and South Korea commit to net zero carbon emissions by 2050.

In Australia: Australia's second wave is over. It is election day in Queensland. The Victorian Premier takes his first day off after 120 consecutive daily press briefings. A giant 500-meter high (~550-yard high) coral reef wall is discovered in the Great Barrier Reef.

In the United States: Amy Coney Barrett's nomination to the Supreme Court is confirmed. The US surpasses 9 million cases. The world speculates about the potential for violence in the immediate aftermath of the coming elections.

Prompt: The upcoming elections in the United States and the raging pandemic are the subjects that grip the week, creating widespread nervousness. How were you feeling this week? Describe your predictions for the election and the course of the COVID19 pandemic.

Dear Fellow Traveller in the year 2020,

You've made it this far and I leave you to take your own notes on real-world events for November and December as you continue describing your personal journey through 2020.

While the weekly prompts end here, I've listed plenty more for you to choose from at the back of the journal.

Your friend in journaling,

Tor Roxburgh

2 Nov - 8 Nov 2020

In the religious year, Hindu women fast during Karva Chauth.

This week's schedule includes the US presidential elections.

9 Nov - 15 Nov 2020

In the religious year, Hindus celebrate Diwali – the festival of lights.

This week's schedule includes Remembrance Day in Australia and Veterans' Day in the US.

16 Nov - 22 Nov 2020

In the religious year, Hindus celebrate brotherhood and sisterhood in the Bhai Dooj festival.

23 Nov - 29 Nov 2020

In the religious year Advent begins for Christians.

This week's schedule includes Thanksgiving Day in the US.

30 Nov - 6 Dec 2020

The seasons turn this week: spring to summer in the Southern Hemisphere; fall to winter in the Northern Hemisphere.

This week's schedule includes the planned easing of restrictions in France and Britain.

7 Dec - 13 Dec 2020

In the religious year, Jews begin celebrating Chanukah – the festival of lights.

This week's schedule obliges all US states to resolve the appointment of their slate of electors.

14 Dec - 20 Dec 2020

In this week's schedule in the US, the electors meet inside their own states to cast their votes for the president and vice president.

21 Dec - 27 Dec 2020

The Northern Hemisphere endures the shortest day of the year this week and in the Southern Hemisphere, the summer solstice brings the longest day. Many people celebrate Christmas Eve and Christmas Day.

In this week's schedule in the US, the electors' votes are given to the US Vice President and other officials.

28 Dec 2020 - 3 Jan 2021

In this week's schedule, the world celebrates New Year's Eve and we all look forward to a better 2021.

Bonus Prompts

Upbeat Prompts

- Describe the person who inspired you this year and explain why.

- Tell your future self about the most exciting event this year.

- What book brought you joy this year and why?

- If you watch television or enjoy movies, describe the most interesting thing you've seen this year.

- What are some of the smaller journeys you took this year? It could be the walks to your coffee shop, to your children's school or something more unusual.

- Describe your most optimistic thought this year.

- Describe your mornings and linger on your favourite rituals.

- How has faith helped you this year?

- What was heart-warming for you this year?

- Describe some of your significant 'firsts' for the year.

- Choose a song that was released this year and describe what it evokes for you.

- Go to your closet and pull out an outfit. Journal about how it ended up with you and where you wore it this year.

- Describe one of your celebrations this year.

- Describe one of your friends and what that person meant to you this year.

Consoling Prompts

- Sacrifices can hurt but remembering their purpose can help. What sacrifices have you been making this year and why?

- Describe an instance this year when you overcame fear and did the right thing.

- Have you acquired a new pet or have your pets brought you comfort this year?

- If you felt worried during this year, how did you keep up your spirits and keep your optimism alive?

- Which people have you enjoyed not seeing this year?

- List three things you've learned in 2020.

- Describe your feelings about the natural world in the context of the pandemic.

- Look out your window and describe something of the world around you. How has the view changed over the course of the year?

COVID19-themed prompts

- Did you enter a second lockdown? What were your thoughts?

- Are you home-schooling children? What was it like?

- How did you celebrate your birthday in 2020?

- The news has been omnipresent in 2020. Describe what you were watching, listening to, reading, and how you coped with news reports.

- Have you given up using cash this year?

- Describe COVID19's impact on your cooking and eating habits.

- Describe COVID19's impact on your exercise regime.

- ✺ Democracy has felt fragile this year. Describe what has been going on in your country.

- ✺ Will you get inoculated when a vaccine has been approved and why?

- ✺ Has the pandemic altered your circle of friends?

- ✺ Which people have you missed seeing this year?

- ✺ How do you feel about world leaders contracting COVID19?

- ✺ If you have children, describe some of the ways they have been reacting to this year's events.

- ✺ Describe how holidays and time off work have been impacted by the pandemic.

- ✺ Look back at your social media feed for this week. Describe the images or words that catch your attention.

- ✺ If you have had a loss this year, describe what happened.

- ✺ How have you become stronger this year?

www.ingramcontent.com/pod-product-compliance
Lightning Source LLC
Chambersburg PA
CBHW060529010526
44110CB00052B/2542